A Sock Is a Pocket for Your Toes

A Pocket Book

by Elizabeth Garton Scanlon

illustrated by Robin Preiss Glasser

HARPERCOLLINSPUBLISHERS

A Sock Is a Pocket for Your Toes
Text copyright © 2004 by Elizabeth Garton Scanlon
Illustrations copyright © 2004 by Robin Preiss Glasser
Manufactured in China by South China Printing Company Ltd. All rights reserved.
www.harperchildrens.com
Library of Congress Cataloging-in-Publication Data
Scanlon, Elizabeth Garton.
A sock is a pocket for your toes: a pocket book / by Elizabeth Garton Scanlon / illustrated
by Robin Preiss Glasser.
p.   cm.
Summary: A poetic celebration of nontraditional pockets and what they hold, pointing out
that a sock is a pocket for your toes and a vase is a pocket for a rose.
ISBN 0-06-029526-0 — ISBN 0-06-029527-9 (lib. bdg.)
1. Pockets—Juvenile poetry.   2. Children's poetry, American.   [1. Pockets—Poetry.
2. American poetry.]   I. Preiss-Glasser, Robin, ill. II. Title.
PS3607 .A78 P63 2004   2001051453
811'.6—dc21   CIP
                                                                              AC
Typography by Matt Adamec   1 2 3 4 5 6 7 8 9 10   ❖   First Edition

For Finlay and Willa, the muses two
—E.G.S.

For Sasha and Benjamin,
who make my pockets so full
—R.P.G.

A sock is a pocket for your toes,

a vase is a pocket
for a rose.

A pocket for a chicken
is a coop,

and a bowl is a pocket full of soup—

uh-oh!

A bowl is a pocket spilling soup.

A cave is a pocket for a bear,

a breath is a pocket
full of air.

A hat is a pocket
for your hair,

and a seat is a pocket called a chair—

please scootch.

This chair is a pocket to be shared.

A pocket for a bird
is a nest,

a bed is a pocket for a rest.

A bathtub is a pocket full of suds,

and piggies love a pocket full of mud—

oink oink.
The piggies need a rub-a-dub-dub.

A lake is a pocket for a duck,

a horseshoe is a pocket
full of luck.

A chimney is a pocket blowing smoke,

and a pocket for a giggle is a joke—
tee hee.

A pocket packed with giggles is a joke.

A phone is a pocket
for a ring,

a bell is a pocket
for a ding.

A pocket for a duckling is a shell,

and a pocket for a farmer is a dell—
_hi ho._

The farmer and his dairy
in the dell.

A pocket for a family
is a home,

a pocket for an ice cream
is a cone.

A poem is a pocket for a rhyme,

and stars are little pockets full of shine—
blink blink.

Wish upon a pocket full of shine.

A pocket for a whisper
is an ear,

a smile is a pocket
of good cheer.

Wide arms are pockets made for hugs,

and your heart is a pocket full of love—
sweet love.

My heart is a pocket full of love.